ISO 50001

A strategic guide to establishing an energy management system

ISO 50001

A strategic guide to establishing an energy management system

ALAN FIELD

IT Governance Publishing

IT Governance Publishing Ltd
Unit 3, Clive Court
Bartholomew's Walk
Cambridgeshire Business Park
Ely, Cambridgeshire
CB7 4EA
United Kingdom
www.itgovernancepublishing.co.uk

© Alan Field 2019

The author has asserted the rights of the author under the Copyright, Designs and Patents Act, 1988, to be identified as the author of this work.

First published in the United Kingdom in 2019 by IT Governance Publishing.

ISBN 978-1-78778-152-8

ABOUT THE AUTHOR

Alan Field, MA, LL.B (Hons), PgC, MCQI CQP, MIIRSM, GIFireE, is a chartered quality professional, an IRCA registered lead auditor and member of The Society of Authors.

Alan has particular expertise in auditing and third-party assessing anti-bribery management systems (ABMSs) to ISO 37001 and BS 10500 requirements, and counter-fraud systems in the public sector to ISO 9001 requirements. He has many years' experience with quality and integrated management systems in the property, engineering, legal and financial sectors. Alan also has experience in auditing, assessment and gap analysis roles within the project management sector.

ACKNOWLEDGEMENTS

I would like to thank Chris Achillea, Roland Tan and Chris J Ward for their time and helpful comments during the production of this book.

CONTENTS

INTRODUCTION

What is an EnMS and why should we invest in one?

This pocket guide gives a practical but strategic overview for leadership teams of what an energy management system (EnMS) is and how implementing one can bring added value to an organisation. It is not a 'how to' book but explains why starting the 'do' is a good strategic decision.

Energy management is, in one sense, not so much about energy but rather the management of resources. This doesn't just apply for the organisation but, ultimately, for the wider world. This is one reason why an EnMS can become part of a broader corporate social responsibility approach.

This book is also a strategic guide to how an EnMS can integrate with an environmental management system (EMS). Many organisations that are considering implementing an EnMS will already have an EMS. An EnMS has similarities to an EMS but there are key differences as well.

So, an EnMS can be about more than the management of energy; it can also support a wider range of sustainable policies, which can be a catalyst for or simply an outcome of developing an EnMS.

An EnMS, effectively implemented, can reduce energy costs, aid strategic thinking about longer-term energy savings, increase energy security and support continual improvement for an EMS, as well the energy management processes themselves. Energy consumption is almost always the servant of the core processes that support the production of goods and services, e.g. what pays the bills and stakeholder dividends.

ISO 50001:2018 (which we will refer to as ISO 50001, although please be aware there is an earlier version of the Standard) is the International Organization for Standardization's (ISO) framework for organisations – both large and small – to manage and reduce their energy use and costs. This pocket guide follows ISO 50001's principles for an EnMS, but can also be read by those who are using other approaches to their EnMS or wider environmental or sustainability issues. IT Governance Publishing also produces pocket guides on standards such as ISO 14001:2015 (the international standard for an EMS)[1] and ISO 9001:2015 (which specifies the requirements for a quality management system (QMS), which can support an EnMS by providing systems for measurement and analysis of data).[2] These pocket guides detail the individual standards' requirements and how they can benefit an organisation. There is also a pocket guide on implementing an integrated management system (IMS),[3] which can help those considering integrating their EMS with an EnMS, as well as other standards.

There are different approaches to energy management, and its importance, whether financial or reputational, to individual organisations varies depending on sector. For example, an EnMS is very relevant to a commercial property management business, where there are a lot of energy-related resources, such as a large estate of office buildings, and where a defined approach to energy management is important to purchasers, tenants and joint venture partners.

If key energy policy insights and objectives are not determined at the outset, the EnMS journey can become unnecessarily slow or even misdirected. This pocket guide can help you start that journey on the right foot by defining policy and strategy at the earliest stage.

ISO 50001 is not a technical standard in the sense of expecting particular technological solutions; each EnMS is different and the way that energy consumption is determined, resourced and improved will be different, even if the techniques used often follow a number of common approaches. Sometimes an EnMS

---

[1] *www.itgovernancepublishing.co.uk/product/iso-14001-step-by-step-a-practical-guide*.

[2] *www.itgovernancepublishing.co.uk/product/iso-9001-2015*.

[3] *www.itgovernancepublishing.co.uk/product/implementing-an-integrated-management-system-ims*.

will place strong emphasis on monitoring and measuring existing energy consumption, while others might focus on substantial changes to processes and technologies with the aim of reducing or adjusting consumption patterns. Many an EnMS will be somewhere in between.

An EnMS can also be implemented or reviewed as part of a more built environment methodology, such as Leadership in Energy and Environmental Design (LEED), which is an approach developed in the US but used globally, and the UK's Building Research Establishment Environmental Assessment Method (BREEAM), which also has wider global acceptance. While these were chiefly devised as sustainable design approaches, design has a significant impact on the long-term operation of a building, and both BREEAM and LEED can be adapted as standalone approaches to an organisation's EnMS. However, both approaches tend to support ISO 50001; LEED, for example, can form the basis of an energy policy and the risk-based approach to energy measurement that ISO 50001 can provide.

So, what is an EnMS?

An EnMS can be defined in a number of ways. This is the Carbon Trust's definition:

> Using energy efficiently helps save money as well as helping to conserve resources and tackle climate change. Adoption of the ISO 50001 standard helps energy performance improvement via the development and use of an energy management system (EnMS) based on a model of continual improvement. It can support the integration of energy management into an environmental improvement strategy.[4]

It is also important to understand what is meant by 'energy management'. Lloyd's Register describes it as follows:

> Energy comes in many forms including electricity, gas, oil and steam, and is a resource used by organisations worldwide. Reducing your energy consumption and

---

[4] *www.carbontrust.com/media/672930/carbon-trust-iso-50001.pdf*.

managing energy efficiency will not only reduce your costs, but will also reduce your carbon footprint and help protect the natural environment. It also reduces your reliance on others to provide the energy you need to operate, hence reducing the risk to your organisation.[5]

Both quotations express concepts that many senior managers will understand immediately – efficiency, performance, environment, carbon footprint, management and continual improvement. However, understanding them in the context of an EnMS requires a more process-based or holistic approach.

The quotations also allude to conserving resources and reducing energy consumption as part of an EnMS. Indirectly these concepts reduce the amount of pollution and waste generated as, ultimately, less energy and/or more efficient sources of energy can be deployed once an EnMS is developed. Such concepts could impact both the environmental and energy policies at strategic level. Even if energy was free, producing, distributing and using it would still have an environmental impact. Renewable energy sources have environmental impacts, even if these are considerably less than fossil fuels.

In other words, using less energy or managing your energy consumption will almost certainly result in less pollution and waste – and an EnMS can help turn good intentions into a reality. This is a key strategic takeaway. Under this sustainable way of thinking, it can also make sense to integrate an EMS with a fledgling EnMS.

This pocket guide will explain how energy aligns with these concepts and how adopting ISO 50001 can be a vehicle to achieving an EnMS.

---

[5] Lloyd's Register, *Energy Management Systems*, "Implementing ISO 50001: 2018".

CHAPTER 1: WHY IS ENERGY MANAGEMENT A STRATEGIC ISSUE?

All organisations need to be more competitive. A part of this is using resources efficiently – lower costs can mean higher profits or, at the very least, more effective product or service delivery. Nothing new in that.

However, energy management is as much about preventing pollution as it is conserving resources. Customers are increasingly aware of wider issues of sustainability – what was 40 years ago the realm of eccentrics is now mainstream and urgent. This is coupled with greater regulation concerning climate change and other environmental matters, which impacts many organisations. Even those who question the validity of climate change cannot deny that fossil fuel energy resources are finite and that world demand for energy is increasing, with parts of the developing world now becoming more industrialised, and consumers expecting a wider range of products.

It is true that some extraction techniques such as fracking increase the timeline of energy stocks, and new technologies such as biogas can create alternative and more sustainable streams of production. However, these all have their own costs and environmental impacts. Some renewable energy sources have a lower carbon footprint but there is no free ride with any energy source, either financially or in terms of sustainability. More importantly, your customers know it.

There are many ways to economise energy use, with a number of technologies and systems available to monitor and reduce consumption. ISO 50001 is a way to bring together energy policies and initiatives into a single management system. 'Clean growth' is a buzz phrase that in essence means better productivity but fewer greenhouse gas emissions. In October 2017, the UK government introduced the Clean Growth Strategy, which recognises the demand for enormous reductions in carbon emissions to combat climate change, together with a need for cleaner air.[6] In some markets, consumers are becoming more aware of the need for decarbonisation (the amount – or average amount – of carbon in primary energy that reduces over a defined period of time), and expect their suppliers of goods and services to recognise it.

One key strategic point to bear in mind is that in terms of ISO 50001 requirements, energy management does not necessarily align with green energy policies, e.g. renewable forms of energy. Energy performance might be improved by such technologies but not in all circumstances.

For example, reducing an organisation's energy demand might reduce national demand on fossil fuel-generated energy, but equally, if an organisation was using renewable energy inefficiently, this could negatively impact the amount of fossil fuels that still need to be used. So, ISO 50001 cannot be seen as just a strategy to support renewables, or as one that supports all renewables without question. Understanding energy consumption and performance means that an organisation looks critically at how it sources its energy; in turn, this might encourage more green sources to be adopted as part of the mix.

It is key to remember that simply saying an organisation will reduce energy consumption does not mean it has an EnMS. Understanding how, why and where energy is being used is essential when devising an EnMS, whatever the motives may be for trying to use less energy.

While some experts might frown at the analogy, there are similarities between waste management policies and energy policies – there is as much a hierarchy of energy consumption as there is waste generation; the ideal waste is that which isn't generated and, equally, instead of using energy reduction as a starting point, it is critical to look at each stage of a process to

---

[6] *https://assets.publishing.service.gov.uk/government/uploads/system/uploads/attachment_data/file/700496/clean-growth-strategy-correction-april-2018.pdf.*

see if fewer resources can be deployed for the same outputs. This where quality and energy management can become bedfellows.

This leads us to another strategic reason for implementing an EnMS – energy security. For example, natural gas sometimes originates from politically unstable areas of the world, so there is a risk supplies could be withdrawn for political reasons. Another example is the use of electric cars – while substantiable in themselves, their recharging requirements will eventually put enormous demand on the National Grid. These are just two examples, but show that energy may not always be available on demand.

All security – be it energy or otherwise – reflects an element of uncertainty that has to be accepted and, where possible, addressed. Looking critically at your organisation's energy consumption today, projecting it over a longer period of time and deciding how these outcomes can be improved not only makes good business sense but also supports resiliency goals for both the organisation and its stakeholders. Or, to put it another way, opportunity cost discussions will now always have energy factored in.

Benefits of an EnMS

- Better understanding of actual energy use on a periodic basis (depending on the process, this might mean by the day or by the second).
- More effective leadership focus on energy flows, e.g. setting energy policy and objectives.
- Better focus of both staff and other interested parties regarding energy use and how it may be more efficiently used.
- Smarter use of energy – unnecessary, excessive or inconsistent consumption can be identified and resolved.
- The risks and opportunities arising from using different energy sources can be examined, including renewable sources.

- Capital investment decisions can take into account energy considerations, e.g. new equipment and/or processes that use less energy or have less carbon impact.

ISO 50001 – is it essential for an EnMS?

The short answer is no. An international standard such as ISO 50001 can provide an effective framework for an EnMS but there are other possibilities, as we will see later.

CHAPTER 2: TERMS AND DEFINITIONS

Annex SL

HLS

ISO 50001 is part of the Annex SL family of ISO standards. In broad terms, ISO's Annex SL high level structure (HLS) does what it says on the tin. It means that all future assessable ISO standards need to follow the high level requirements outlined in Annex SL.

Annex SL should be read as a document and not just consulted – even if the proposed EnMS doesn't follow ISO standards.

For a leadership team member, arguably it is more important to read Annex SL than the standard itself (although, ideally, both should be read). This is because the approach taken with the HLS can assist with defining strategic ideas. It might also provoke other ideas within some organisations – for example, is risk-based thinking the only approach to take with energy management?

Annex SL assumes that continual improvement is the goal of every organisation because it assumes that a Plan-Do-Check-Act (PDCA) model is a core approach to process management (more about this later). Annex SL also assumes that all management systems are leadership led and managed, and that risk-based thinking is used throughout the PDCA model.

Since 2012, many new versions of ISO standards – such as ISO 9001 and ISO 14001 – have been issued incorporating Annex SL requirements. One intended output of this is that an organisation will find it more straightforward to create an IMS as the HLS will be the same across all standards.

So, for example, an organisation with ISO 14001:2015 and ISO 50001:2018 will now be working to a common HLS even though both these standards have different requirements. This is why ISO 14001 and ISO 50001 can, in many respects, be integrated or otherwise aligned. Again, we will look at this possibility more later.

HLS clauses

Annex SL provides the HLS for all future accessible management systems that ISO agrees. This includes ISO 50001. The HLS has ten elements, or clauses, that are common across all Annex SL standards.

1. **Scope** – this relates the intended outcome of the management system. In practice, it provides the parameters and any limitations of what the management system will include.

2. **Normative references** – this provides details of the publications and reference standards that the management system will be subject to – in reality, something many strategic managers will have explained to them by their technical managers!

3. **Terms and definitions** – this states any specific terms and definitions applicable to the individual ISO standard concerned, e.g. ISO 50001. Again, something strategic managers will have explained to them by their technical managers if applicable to wider energy management decisions.

4. **Context of the organisation** – this details the organisation's place in the marketplace, and how its vision, governance and goals fit in with the scope of the management system. Each Annex SL standard, including ISO 50001, explains more about the context in relation to its requirements.

5. **Leadership** – all Annex SL standards are leadership based – in practice, middle managers only support the leadership involvement with the management system. Before Annex SL, many ISO standards only expected top management involvement with setting and reviewing policy and objectives, rather than the entire management system. As

this pocket guide focuses on the reasons behind strategic decision making, the implication of the leadership requirements of Annex SL is inherent in all of the contents.

6. **Planning** – in Annex SL, planning equates to risks and opportunities. While planning a management system may involve many strategic and even tactical considerations, the risk-based approach to management is the key consideration. Leadership must define objectives for minimising risk and maximising opportunities, and put a management system in place to support them. The whole management system operates and is measured according to these objectives, which is why defining them is a planning requirement.

7. **Support** – is what it says on the tin. People, infrastructure, communications and documented information. The need for human resources is based on competence, awareness and communication – are these adequate for meeting the requirements of the management system? With ISO 50001, competence can include the risks of not being able to identify, analyse and measure the energy consumption data. These will all require different skills and experience, although IT infrastructure is taking a lot of the donkey work out of such activities. In other words, the way human and physical resources interplay needs to be considered by leadership in a risk-based management system.

8. **Operations** – the day-to-day delivery of management system requirements. These include both in-house and outsourced processes, and process controls such as planned and unplanned changes to achieve a conforming process delivery. All operations' processes directly support the risk-based objectives or, to put it another way, tactical processes are directly aligned with more strategic ones.

9. **Performance evaluation** – this is formed of five key areas: monitoring, measurement, analysis and evaluation,

internal audit and management review. Organisations need to decide how their risk-based management system will be monitored, i.e. measured, analysed and evaluated; these may be comparatively straightforward measures or very complex depending on the size of the organisation, and the breadth of the processes concerned and the level of risk they present. Internal audit is part of this process to ensure the management system continues to conform to the requirements of the organisation as well as the standard applicable, e.g. ISO 50001. Management review looks at whether the management system continues to be effective in minimising risks and maximising opportunities and decides if the current objectives need any amendment.

10. **Continual improvement** – one of the cornerstones of PDCA. The process is circular – the organisation learns from its successes and mistakes and builds the corrective action into future management system planning and objectives. Remember, Annex SL talks about continual and not continuous improvement. 'Continuous' implies a constant and uninterrupted state of improvement, whereas 'continual' means improvement over a long period of time. The monitoring and measurement processes are there to identify where improvement has been achieved and, of course, where corrective actions are needed, but these corrective actions, if successful in their implementation, lead to continual improvement as well.

Leadership

Perhaps the most important Annex SL clause is leadership. Annex SL requires management systems to be leadership led. This has always been the case with some alternative (or complementary) models to ISO standards, such as the EFQM Excellence Model.

The leadership approach was a big change for organisations that had management systems such as ISO 14001:2004, that had been left chiefly to middle management to run after signing off on high-level policies. In broad terms, the organisations that already had a leadership model for their management systems found transition to the 2015 version of ISO 14001 more straightforward. A similar process is ongoing with those that have ISO 50001:2011 and are beginning (or completing) their transitions to the 2018 version of the Standard. The leadership approach will be very similar – or identical if the EMS and EnMS are integrated.

One key issue with an IMS is that even if leadership responsibility is shared between a number of individuals at board level, there needs to be some coordination to ensure a meaningful level of integration – otherwise the management system is only combined. This coordination is either from, or championed by, top management.

The next chapter discusses leadership engagement before and during EnMS implementation, but one broader point to keep in mind is that the risk-based thinking requirements of Annex SL should create interest within top management and leadership – deciding upon and managing risks relating to the EnMS is within their sphere of decision-making and is not just a middle-management concern.

PDCA

PDCA was a cornerstone of ISO standards long before Annex SL was introduced. The way PDCA works needs to be understood because it can provide an existing – and very effective – focus on the way an organisation moves towards an IMS.

PDCA is sometimes known as the Deming Cycle after the American quality guru W. Edwards Deming (1900–1993), or the Shewart Cycle after another American, the engineer and statistician Walter A. Shewhart (1891–1967). Today, the Shewhart Cycle typically refers to a statistical process control version of PDCA – hence why the Deming Cycle can be seen as a more generic application of the approach.

In short, PDCA is a circular approach to management – we plan, communicate and mobilise a process, then:

- Undertake the process (or processes), including making minor adjustments;
- Check if the process has performed as anticipated (this, of course, could be under or overperformance). This is the check phase (sometimes called the learning phase or after action review). Once we understand why performance variations occurred, the leadership team can decide a way forward, including how to prevent reoccurrence of the process variation; and
- Act (or standardise or calibrate) the process. This is based on the outcome of the check phase. This phase forms part of the continual improvement approach and is fed back into the plan phase of the cycle.

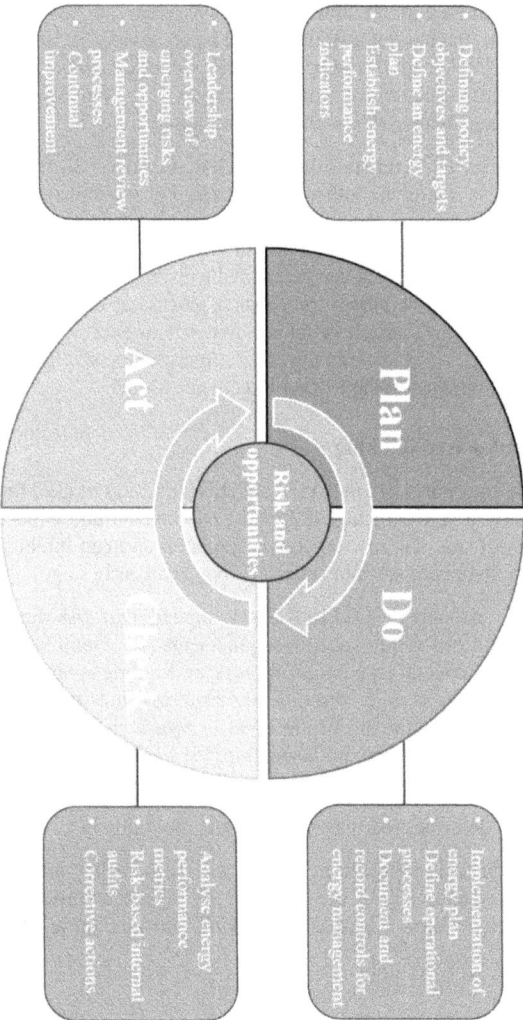

Figure 1: The PDCA cycle

The PDCA cycle diagram with four quadrants:

Plan
- Defining policy, objectives and targets
- Define an energy plan
- Establish energy performance indicators

Do
- Implementation of energy plan
- Define operational processes
- Document and record controls for energy management

Check
- Analyse energy performance metrics
- Risk-based internal audits
- Corrective actions

Act
- Leadership overview of emerging risks and opportunities
- Management review process
- Continual improvement

Risk and opportunities

It doesn't mean, however, that continual improvement can't be determined in in other ways; PDCA should be seen as an umbrella and not a straitjacket. The creativity that arises out of not having to slavishly following a checklist of requirements means that wider corporate goals can be aligned with management systems' implementation goals.

While PDCA remains the bedrock of all Annex SL standards, it is also useful for other approaches. For example, the **Check** phase aligns well with Six Sigma and Lean approaches, while the **Plan** and **Act** phases can be aligned with EFQM-type approaches. PDCA can be aligned with an EnMS in a number of ways, such as energy purchasing processes, designing energy performance targets or taking evidence of energy conservation as part of implementing the corporate social responsibility requirements of the EFQM Excellence Model.

Risk-based thinking

Before Annex SL, the ISO standards that could be used for third-party assessment had different requirements and expectations about risk. This is sometimes forgotten and can inhibit EnMS implementation if not reflected upon at an early stage.

For example, ISO 14001:2004 implied that risk had to be considered within specific requirements (for example, defining environmental aspects and impacts, or deciding upon emergency preparedness and response procedures) but there was no requirement for the whole EMS to take a risk-based thinking approach, directed by leadership. ISO 14001:2015, drafted in accordance with Annex SL, completely changed this.

ISO describes risk-based thinking as the following:

> Risk is inherent in all aspects of a quality management system. There are risks in all systems, processes and functions. Risk-based thinking ensures these risks are

identified, considered and controlled throughout the design and use of the quality management system.[7]

The complicated bit is whether the organisation accepts risk-based thinking as an approach and what it sees as risks and opportunities within its management systems, in this case its EnMS.

What an organisation sees as risks it recognises or wishes to treat can vary considerably. For some organisations, the cost of energy or understanding the performance of assets consuming energy will be the main focus, while in others reducing their carbon footprint is the main driver, e.g. Energy Savings Opportunity Scheme (ESOS) compliance. As with any strategy, top management needs clear goals and direction – one size or one approach does not fit all.

The notion of exploiting opportunities and minimising risk sounds obvious but often isn't. This can be a challenge when implementing a management system, especially with energy performance, where there may be a complex melange of technical, financial, compliance and infrastructure implications for a leadership team to understand and consider. Tactics may follow strategy but, with an EnMS, the detail will often impact on energy policy.

Where an organisation already has a detailed approach to risk management, aligning this with risk-based thinking may seem simple. For example, risk registers or enterprise risk management-type systems often look at the whole organisation and not at risks in silos. Indeed, the headache can be deciding what risks the EnMS will influence or control rather than the wider financial and political risks that these risk register-type systems will often assume.

---

[7]*https://committee.iso.org/files/live/sites/tc176sc2/files/documents/ISO%209001%202015%20-%20Implementation%20guidance%20docs/ISO9001_2015_and_Risk.docx*.

However, it is important to bear in mind that, in the context of Annex SL, risks mean uncertainty in meeting agreed objectives (although some individual standards have tweaked this a little). Thinking in silos isn't just functional – it can be encouraged by standards being interpreted as creating their own special universe that nothing and no one can impact. Arguably, until very recently, this is how some leadership teams looked at energy management – as a set of inevitable outcomes: increased consumption and pollution. Planning for an EnMS can help dispel such views and can show that continual improvement is achievable by applying a systems based approach to energy management.

These examples also help a leadership team understand that an integrated approach reduces uncertainty.

So, there is a 'chicken and egg' element. With an IMS, objectives can't be agreed until the organisation's own view of risk is understood; equally, the uncertainties an organisation really wants to avoid will drive decisions on objectives. One example might be the need to drive down reject rates of a product; there are risks and opportunities (or benefits) with investing in this strategy but if the issue is ignored, the risk to sales, reputation and rework budgets could be critical. This can also have a significant impact on energy consumption and any subsequent pollution as both the rejects and the rework use energy.

So, it is for leadership to decide where its focus is going to be, which might be partly driven not just by customers but other stakeholders' expectations (known as interested parties under Annex SL).

Equally, the targets or other outcomes an organisation really wants to achieve can form at least part of the opportunities aspects of objectives, e.g. better control over energy usage, or energy performance indicators (EnPIs) showing more rapid improvement than originally planned for. Without monitoring and measuring processes it would be difficult to quantify any changes – hence why Annex SL also requires these processes.

Key terminology of an EnMS

It can be helpful to explain some of the terminology used by experts when discussing energy management and the link with an EMS. The list is not exhaustive but it does aid the decision-making process when expert advice is being given or sought, along with reading the content of this pocket guide.

While the terminology defined chiefly relates to ISO 50001, it could be adapted to other forms of EnMS.

Energy management system (EnMS)

ISO says that the aim of ISO 50001 is:

> To enable organizations to establish the systems and processes necessary to continually improve energy performance, including energy efficiency, energy use and energy consumption.[8]

That isn't a bad definition of an EnMS either. If the organisation already has ISO 9001 or ISO 14001 certification, the terms, systems, processes and continual improvement will often align with those principles. Also, ISO 9001 and ISO 14001 are performance-based management systems, as is ISO 50001.

ISO 50001 refers specifically to "energy performance culture", and ISO proposes that an EnMS should have an energy performance approach. This assumes a systematic, data-driven suite of processes focused on continually improving energy consumption and performance. In reality, it is difficult to implement an EnMS that is not data driven if only because, without metrics, the advantages of understanding energy consumption and energy are not going to be achieved.

Risk and opportunities

Under most Annex SL standards, the notion of risks and opportunities can be seen as the effect of uncertainty. This might

---

[8] ISO 50001:2018, Standard Introduction, 0.1 General.

be the threats of adverse deviation from planned outcomes, or opportunities arising from unanticipated beneficial outcomes. Unplanned outcomes relate to events or outcomes; for example, a new bit of kit that didn't arrive on time or improvement targets that weren't met. So, risks and opportunities provide a wide canvas to define more precise definitions for an organisation's circumstances.

Clause 6.1 of ISO 50001 places risk and opportunities under 'Planning' and is explicitly linked to performance, i.e. the risks and opportunities of not achieving or overachieving within the objectives set by leadership relating to energy efficiency, energy use and energy consumption. It is for each leadership team to identify and prioritise risks and opportunities and make the best decision for the organisation at that time. This aligns very closely with most EMSs, especially if the environmental aspects and impacts include energy management factors.

Interested parties

In all Annex SL standards, there are interested parties who are not customers, contractors or owners. An interested party is anyone with an expectation of the organisation's EnMS, including its legal and regulatory requirements. So, interested parties can include regulators, investors, holding companies or associated companies that are not part of the EnMS, neighbours, and others. This is very similar to an EMS in concept and scope. To actively identify and consider interested parties can have a number of unexpected benefits – for example, investors or associated companies not directly involved in an EnMS may influence continual improvement through their different ways of managing energy. Regulators are more than finger waggers and can propose initiatives or even encourage benchmarking activities.

Context of the organisation

Another Annex SL idea. In simple terms, context of the organisation sits above energy policy, in other words, what should drive policy is the expectations of interested parties (particularly owners, customers and regulators), the state of the marketplace, changes in technology and anything else that impacts the existence of the organisation – whether private, public or not for profit. Some organisations will use standard management techniques such as a SWOT Analysis to identify, among other things, how significant energy is to the organisation. With ISO 14001, this includes all applicable aspects of environmental management; an EnMS has a narrower focus. However, they are entirely compatible and an integrated context of the organisation approach is complementary.

Energy performance indicators (EnPIs)

Energy performance relates to measurable standards of energy use, performance and consumption. The measurable standard or metric is based on an organisation's objectives and energy targets. In turn, EnPIs are defined by each organisation's measure or unit of performance. This may be clear-cut or open to interpretation depending on the energy policy and objectives being achieved.

Once agreed, EnPIs need to be understood by the leadership team for consistent understanding of the implications for other energy decisions taken.

Energy baselines (EnBs)

EnBs are reference points from which comparisons can be made of energy performance. These might be based on time period or different parts of process cycles. Different EnBs might be defined for the purposes of energy performance improvement goals, e.g. with or without an improvement being implemented. It should also be remembered that there are always **static factors**, i.e. factors that do not routinely change, which need to be understood before EnPIs and EnBs are understood. Furthermore, there can be no EnBs or any specific EnPIs without an **energy review (EnR).** This is unique to every organisation but will be based on fairly standard techniques. The EnR will determine current and any historic energy sources across all processes and sites, including areas of significant energy use. Depending on its outcome, there may be changes to energy policy and objectives; the EnR will often show areas of unidentified energy usage and even, in some cases, that the organisation's total energy spend has not been fully identified in budgets.

CHAPTER 3: INTEGRATING ISO 50001 AND ISO 14001 – THE STRATEGIC ADVANTAGE

ISO 50001 and ISO 14001 – the benefits of integration

In strategic terms, an IMS is an integration of all of an organisation's processes and system working under – and towards – one set of policies and objectives. In other words, risk and opportunities are no longer managed in silos within the organisation but, instead, with one unified, or integrated, approach from the leadership team. There is less duplication, less waste of resources and a more focused approach to managing issues and opportunities. Sounds too good to be true? It depends on the organisation's goals and the way it is currently managed, especially at senior and middle management levels.

Less duplication and waste of resources sounds very ISO 50001 and, indeed, very ISO 14001. In other words, with good planning, not only are there going to be resource savings from implementing both standards, but even more savings can be achieved by looking at how controlling energy consumption fits in so well with a wider environmental or sustainability policy.

With an EMS and EnMS, the unified approach seems, on the face of it, logical because of the similarity of subject matter. However, any pitfalls, as well as the many advantages, need to be examined before a decision is taken to use resources to implement an IMS.

The decision to implement an IMS should be leadership led – the leadership team will need to take ownership of the process and there may even be some internal conflicts along the way. The decision to implement an integrated ISO 14001 and ISO 50001 management system could be motivated by the need to minimise risk; to support corporate responsibility to improve environmental and energy performance for contractual or reputational enhancement; to provide greater efficiency in terms of cost; or to simplify administrative processes or functional structures.

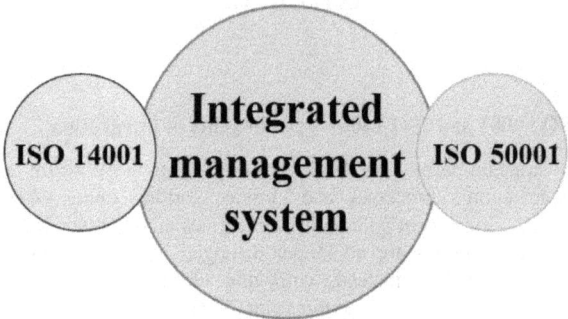

Figure 2: An integrated management system

Let us look at two specific examples. First, a risk-based approach to environmental management to support ISO 14001:2015 might have a substantial element relating to energy management opportunities, such as reducing CO_2 emissions, and risks such as exceeding planned energy consumption. So, creating a common risk-based approach to meet both ISO 14001 and ISO 50001 expectations may not be a great stretch.

Another possible driver for integration could be corporate responsibility policies. Some organisations keep these separate from other management systems, while others integrate them into their EMS. Indeed, energy management might be seen as part of this, especially if corporate responsibility is seen as more than supporting local initiatives, for example, supporting decarbonisation or other global sustainability issues. The imperative to do this might increase if the organisation already has a management system that would provide a level of recognition for these different levels of continual improvement, e.g. SA 8000, which is an auditable certification standard (overseen by Social Accountability Accreditation Services in New York) and encourages organisations to develop, maintain and apply socially acceptable practices in the workplace. The EFQM Excellence Model requires, among other elements, that the organisation's corporate social responsibility (CSR) is expressed in its values and integrated in the organisation. If an organisation has either of these standards, it can be quite straightforward to extend sustainability and accountability to energy management. But, equally, an organisation might take a policy decision that keeps ISO 50001 as a separate matter.

In addition to the EFQM Excellence Model, the other products that might lend themselves to energy management in terms of integration would be Six Sigma or Lean. There is also ISO 9001, where energy management is intrinsically tied up with core process improvement, for example removing the need for energy by removing a stage of the process; using different – and more energy-efficient machines – to complete stages of the process; changing the process in some way, such as reducing the temperatures required in some stages of a process; or simplifying logistics so that less fuel and/or less vehicles are needed for distribution. EFQM, Lean, Six Sigma and ISO 9001 all focus in their own way on planning and measuring process improvement. At the outset, this could include the requirements of an EnMS, e.g. conducting an EnR, calculating energy costs from which target metrics of improvement can be measured (very Six Sigma), planning leadership processes to champion their improvement (very EFQM), and identifying potential improvements to the processes that generate the EnB itself (very Lean).

Another potential aim of an IMS might be to simplify the monitoring and measurement processes in place. This will particularly appeal to organisations that use Lean- or Six Sigma-type processes (be this formally or just as an influence).

These examples show how a more integrated approach to efficiency can cut across process and functionality; energy can be a key component of processes, rather than just a silo to be managed separately. Alternatively, some organisations will see environmental management as including the policy, monitoring and measurement for energy management, even if core process improvements are seen by that leadership team as a different silo of responsibility.

As we've already mentioned, being 'green' is no longer seen as just a continual improvement goal; many consumers and B2B customers expect organisations to have sustainable credentials. The decision is whether your marketplace sees energy efficiency and/or the impact of energy consumption on carbon footprint as a key interest or concern. If so, then ensuring the EMS aligns with the EnMS may be an investment well worth costing and considering.

An IMS is often an ongoing integration of the management systems that support the organisation. Creating an IMS isn't an instant process. Rarely is it achieved by rigidly sticking to one particular system or approach; it will often be influenced by the good, the bad and occasionally rather mediocre aspects of the different management systems that make up the proposed IMS. These might include an EnMS, EMS, QMS and business continuity management (BCM), among others. These could also be integrated with corporate responsibility (sometimes known as corporate social responsibility), or a wider business ethics approach. Even more common is integrating just two or three of these systems under one set of objectives and leadership responsibilities – with an EMS and EnMS, where objectives have been designed in tandem, this is an obvious approach to consider.

Where a leadership team's motive for implementing an IMS for the EMS and EnMS is continual improvement, the exact improvements being sought need to be defined up front, even if these strategic goals later evolve into rather different priorities or enhancements. This will almost certainly include an element of energy management. The strategic goals are the compass for the journey; some may be energy focused and others more focused on different areas of sustainability. Without them, resources can be diverted into unnecessary detours, rather than progressing the integration goals.

Should an EMS and EnMS be combined or integrated?

One halfway house to implementing an IMS is a combined management system. The combined approach reflects an organisation that sees advantage in operating its risk management system in silos but where there is a level of integration or common systems in some elements. For example, while different board directors might be responsible for the EnMS and the EMS, there are some integrated elements, e.g. objectives, risk assessments, documented information or internal audit processes, or any combination of these.

Many an IMS will begin as a combined system that eventually becomes integrated as all management system elements become fused. Indeed, a management systems assessor will often need to judge if a management system has actually been integrated – rather than just combined – by how far a combined system has achieved integration.

So, the real distinction between integrated and combined approaches is not binary – integration is a journey and may take time to fully achieve, with resources devoted to it. An organisation needs to explicitly decide it wants to take this step. It is not just something nice to have.

In short, there are many advantages to integrating an EnMS with other risk-based or metric-based management systems.

Or, to put it another way, ask yourself why it is better to keep your EnMS in a silo.

CHAPTER 4: A BRIEF OVERVIEW OF WHAT AN EnMS WILL REQUIRE

'Requires' sounds a resource-heavy word. The secret with an EnMS is to implement requirements so they deliver continual improvements but with resources proportionate to the potential benefits.

This chapter explains some of the key deliverables and quick wins an EnMS can deliver once implementation begins. The detail of how this can be achieved may be more technical, but this chapter gives the strategic case for beginning the EnMS journey. The following isn't an exhaustive list but shows the main advantages.

Reducing energy consumption

The word 'reducing' always has a nice ring to it. Less use of resources might mean more profit or, at least, more competitive pricing. However, to reduce energy consumption we need to be able to measure it. Particularly in large, complex organisations, one of the biggest benefits of an EnMS is being able to identify energy spend. One might argue that, through checking the purchase ledgers, we can calculate what we are spending on gas, electricity and other energy sources, e.g. diesel. However, that doesn't tell you if all that is really necessary spending or precisely where it is being spent – we may be heating buildings when they are empty, leaving production machinery on unnecessarily, etc. EnRs and processes such as EnBs calculate energy consumption down to individual process levels, helping to quantify unnecessary energy usage and providing a basis for continual improvement in energy consumption.

Communication

An EnMS encourages management communication because it requires it. This is true of all Annex SL standards – matters not usually questioned or queried are, which generally leads to more efficiency than bureaucracy. A simple example might be identifying that a building management system (BMS) is being used; highlighting this in an EnR means reduced energy usage, better reporting and metrics and, in some cases, less wear and tear on machinery such as air conditioning chillers. Using a BMS properly might even lead to energy reduction and reduced energy bills, with little or no additional cost.

At a more strategic level, not only is the leadership team more focused on energy management, but the metrics required for an EnB also mean there will be clearer horizontal and vertical communication across all levels of management.

As is often the case with an EMS, an EnMS encourages communication among staff, which will raise more awareness of the need to conserve energy, both at local and global levels. This staff involvement can also encourage continual improvement in energy and environmental management.

Technical solutions

One common misconception about an EnMS is that it is all about technical solutions. This can be true, but depends on the organisation; sometimes using current systems more effectively is the best approach, and, as we've seen, there is also much to be gained from understanding energy usage and defining metrics to support improvement.

That said, there are a few broad areas where technical solutions might be appropriate. The obvious one, mentioned before, is that we actually use less energy. This might involve new equipment or better monitoring of energy use, which, in turn, might require technical investment.

For example, as a part of an EnR, it is discovered that inefficient energy use is due to the equipment being used. This could be that LED lighting isn't being used (which can be up to 95% more energy efficient than other lighting methods, depending on the application). Another example is older air conditioning equipment is being used. There could be even more complex changes involving replacing production machinery. The key point is an EnMS will typically look for operational efficiencies first. Investment decisions might be influenced or informed by it, but an EnMS doesn't drive investment decisions.

Another technical solution might be changing the source of energy being used, for example moving towards renewable electricity rather than using gas appliances. Again, there are investment decisions involved. Opportunity, cost and other factors are involved, as with any investment decision, and it is sometimes better to try to achieve more efficiency from existing solutions. Also, deciding to only use renewable sources of energy needs careful thought. For example, does 'renewable' include nuclear energy? How does your organisation verify that the supplier really sources their energy from renewable sources or, rather, how do they define renewable energy?

Finally, the solution might be to use more renewable technologies in day-to-day processes, for example moving to an office building that is designed not to be dependent on artificial heating or cooling sources – sometimes known as an 'eco building'. However, this is not a requirement of an EnMS and a big investment decision. Conversely, if a LEED and BREEAM approach is being followed then it may become a cornerstone of the EnMS.

Starting to implement an EnMS can bring all of the above possibilities to the executive table, which, in itself, might be a reason to consider implementing the EnMS.

CHAPTER 5: HOW AN EMS CAN SUPPORT AN EnMS

From a strategic perspective, an EMS is probably better understood than an EnMS – particularly by those working to ISO 14001:2015 principles.

Implementing an EnMS can seem daunting but, as discussed in chapter three, an IMS can be considered. Even if it isn't, looking at how an EMS can support the EnMS and vice versa makes good business sense. It is not so much reinventing the wheel, rather, using EMS processes already implemented to support energy management policies and targets.

One starting point is to examine to what extent energy is considered in the current EMS. There will certainly be some reference to it even if, say, waste minimisation, biodiversity or minimising the use of chemicals is seen as the priority. If energy consumption or energy minimisation is seen as a key aspect, then the road to an EnMS may not be so long.

We already know that an EnMS is usually systems-based and involves analysing and managing energy usage, so initially, continual improvement can be seen as a smarter deployment of energy resources. In some EnMSs, this can simply be not using unnecessary energy (an example would be identifying that lighting is left on during the night), while at the other end of the scale would be identifying more fundamental process improvements that require less energy, e.g. producing a product using less energy in the process. However, many an EnMS will focus on the more efficient use of energy supporting current processes, i.e. identifying actual energy use and then identifying better ways to deploy it. With an EMS, an organisation is also finding better ways to deploy other resources as well as lessening its impact on the environment – which, of course, energy is part of.

What are the differences and similarities between an EnMS and EMS?

As discussed earlier, Annex SL applies to a number of assessable standards, including ISO 50001 and ISO 14001. Almost any number of Annex SL products could be integrated to create a single set of policies, risk- and opportunity-based objectives, and other leadership-based systems.

There are differences between ISO 14001 and ISO 50001. ISO 14001 is a more generalist standard in terms of environmental management, so top management defines the key risks and opportunities relating to their EMS. In some instances this might be energy, but in others it might be areas such as waste management. ISO 50001, meanwhile, is focused on energy management. However, the risks and opportunities of energy consumption can influence the metrics about wider issues of resource management that an EMS will always focus upon.

Integrating management systems is not a requirement. They can be managed separately. However, is there an advantage in doing this? The current management structure will influence the decision. This could be dictated by differing managerial responsibilities for the EMS and EnMS – for example, there may be an EMS manager but the facilities manager deals with energy matters. And that is before considering the number of board members involved in environmental and energy issues. However, once competitive advantage is identified through at least a level of integration, then an agreed plan for the whole of the EMS, including energy, can be devised.

One approach is to ask the board if it considers energy issues to be part of the environmental policy. The answer is almost certainly yes, although there may be differences of opinion as to the extent of influence. For example, most will agree that the organisation's energy consumption impacts on CO_2 emissions, so planning to reduce or minimise consumption of energy from fossil fuels is both an EMS and EnMS concern.

Consider for a moment some of the terms explained in chapter two. If ISO 50001 principles are adopted, then a documented EnR is required. This isn't required by ISO 14001 but provides useful information to support carbon management, through the analysis of energy use and current energy efficiency being achieved. The data and any other information used, in turn, enables areas of significant energy use to be defined. The extent and detail of this will depend on the organisation and its carbon footprint, which may enable opportunities for energy performance improvement to be identified.

Once identified, areas of significant energy use can be analysed. This might include immediate physical changes (such as installing more sub-metering). It might mean ensuring any BMS is producing all applicable reports – for example, is air conditioning working as efficiently as we imagine? Do we understand variables in our energy consumption, such as hot weather or busy production times when more energy will be needed? Key business costs as well as the strategies to achieve them are also important to sustainable goals. Carbon isn't just produced by the office, factory or warehouse – the energy needs to be obtained from somewhere, and even green energy sources will normally have some (albeit limited) impact on carbon footprint. Just as with waste management, the ideal solution is not to generate the waste in the first place or to generate as little as possible. The same with energy consumption; minimising energy consumption is almost always better than using more from green sources. And less energy purchased means, of course, less of an impact on the bottom line.

All the above information feeds into an EnB. The EnB acts as a starting point to determine current energy use, so future improvement strategies can be measured in terms of success or otherwise. As the EnB matures, it also enables competing strategies or ideas to be more accurately measured in terms of success or impact in return for investment, or base metrics to measure all future improvements in energy consumption or other energy management improvements.

None of this is light years away from an EMS or even a production management system. Energy management, for some organisations, is a bit of mystery, but once understood very little needs to be done to achieve management buy in as the outcomes if not the processes are already understood.

CHAPTER 6: ISO 50001 – THE KEY DIFFERENCES BETWEEN 2011 AND 2018

For those already familiar with ISO 50001:2011, this chapter explains the key differences between the 2011 and 2018 versions of the Standard that would be of immediate interest to a strategic manager.

For those seeking third-party certification, UKAS-approved certification bodies will only accept assessment applications for the 2018 version. Those with ISO 50001:2011 certificates will have to undertake transition assessments to the 2018 version. The assessment process itself is discussed more in the next chapter.

The key differences

ISO 50001:2018 is based on Annex SL (please see chapter two) and follows the HLS approach that Annex SL defines. The 2011 version of ISO 50001 doesn't. When looking at the differences between the two versions, referring to the Annex SL principles will clarify most points.

An organisation with ISO 50001:2011 may already meet some 2018 version requirements, such as a high degree of leadership involvement in the EnMS. While some organisations implement a management system just to meet an assessment requirement, others will implement it to meet their own requirements and expectations. In other words, transition to the 2018 version of ISO 50001 isn't necessarily complex, depending on individual circumstances.

There is a new clause for understanding the organisation and its context. An organisation shall determine external and internal issues relevant to its purpose and that affect its ability to achieve the intended outcomes of its EnMS and improve its energy performance. If you have the 2015 version of ISO 9001 or ISO 14001 this new requirement will be familiar. It can be seen as something sitting above a policy statement – a high-level understanding of the influential factors affecting, positively as well as negatively, energy performance and the EnMS of the organisation. With an EMS, there will be at least an element of energy management when determining these issues.

There is a new clause referring to the systematic determination of the needs and expectations of interested parties – again, those who have the 2015 version of ISO 14001 or ISO 9001 will be familiar with the rationale behind this. This means that interested parties relevant to energy performance and the EnMS need to be identified, along with their needs and expectations of the EnMS from a high-level perspective. Determining needs and expectations of interested parties may not be as straightforward as it first seems and may require strategic direction.

There are also new requirements to demonstrate and engage leadership commitment to support the EnMS, which we have discussed in detail throughout this pocket guide.

Another new process, again discussed at length in this guide, is risk- and opportunity-based strategic decision-making on the EnMS. This is complementary to the EnR, which is a more detailed operational review to define the control and improvement strategies to support energy performance, i.e. it is based on risks and opportunities defined by the leadership team. This approach also includes requirements such as agreeing action plans, EnPIs and EnBs as well as an energy data collection plan. Previously a risk-based approach to management may not have been taken.

There are changes to competency requirements for those whose work impacts on energy performance and the EnMS, including the need to evaluate the effectiveness of actions taken to acquire that necessary competence.

There are also a number of specific changes, including some new definitions of energy performance improvement, EnR and introducing the concept of the normalisation of EnPIs.

Perhaps the most significant change is that preventive action is no longer required, as the risk-based approach to management means, according to ISO's thinking, that areas of shortfall are not corrective actions but could become so – in other words, uncertainty is treated as a risk.

There is also more of an emphasis on root cause analysis, i.e. determining the actual reason why a corrective action has arisen, how that risk can be removed and any opportunities exploited in delivering that process or service in the future; again, uncertainty is managed as a risk or an opportunity depending what the root cause analysis indicates.

CHAPTER 7: THIRD-PARTY ASSESSMENT

This final chapter considers the pros and cons of third-party certification to ISO 50001. Remember that while the certification body (CB) cannot provide consultancy, it can give feedback on how the transition process is progressing and, for an extra fee, provide a gap analysis audit to advise how close your organisation's EnMS is to meeting ISO 50001 requirements. However, this is something an organisation can often do itself by asking the right questions internally.

If an organisation already has, say, ISO 9001 and/or ISO 14001 certification, the external assessment of ISO 50001 can be comparatively straightforward, and the organisation can approach its CB to schedule an assessment, either as a standalone ISO 50001 assessment or an IMS assessment for, say, ISO 14001 with ISO 50001.

However, if an organisation is starting from scratch, the decision as to which CB to choose is more complex.

The key determinant with any assessment product is to decide why you want to do it in the first place. Organisations should beware of consultants or assessment bodies persuading them to have external assessments before they understand the pros and cons.

Drifting into assessment is not worth considering because there are the even greater ongoing commitments of time and resources to maintain certification. It is not like passing your driving test. There will always be regular assessments (sometimes called surveillance or continuing assessments). The end of the world is never nigh in certification (although an organisation can sometimes have its certificate removed by its CB, surrender it itself or change its CB).

However, that said, many organisations believe that without external assessment they would not progress with continual improvement to the same degree. Certification encourages organisations to stay up to speed with changes as any good assessor will expect them to. Instead of being a chore, certification can be used as positive driver for change. The other extreme would be to decide that you simply want a certificate to show to customers – these organisations tend to find maintaining certification difficult as they are being asked to prove things that they have no interest in doing. There has to be a strategic reality check early on as to the motives for spending time and, therefore, money on implementing and maintaining an assessable management system.

With ISO 50001, successful external assessment can be used by organisations to show their ESOS compliance. As this pocket guide has shown, adopting an EnMS to ISO 50001 has other benefits.

Some CBs – if they already assess the organisation for two or more standards – can issue a certificate saying the organisation is now operating an IMS to these standards (after successful assessment). All this means is that the organisation has moved from managing its management systems separately or combined to an integrated approach. Of course, an organisation does need to show it has achieved this. A reputable CB will never rubber stamp such a significant change.

The assessment process

In the UK, while there is no obligation to do so, many stakeholders will only accept an ISO 50001 certificate if the CB is regulated by the United Kingdom Accreditation Service (UKAS). There are non-regulated certification bodies, but their certificates may not be recognised by an organisation's customers or other stakeholders. Furthermore, as UKAS approves CBs on a product-by-product basis, there will be some that are approved for, say, ISO 9001 but not ISO 50001. It is therefore important to check that a CB is UKAS registered, and that it is approved for ISO 50001 – this can be done on the UKAS website.[9]

CBs can have different processes for new clients and existing ones, especially for IMS assessments. So, the choice of CB is not just based on cost but how its requirements and processes fit into the organisation's expectations.

The CB should explain the assessment process in detail and the fees involved. Although it will not be able to provide consultancy, it can recommend consultants or provide quotes for training services.

As fees and expenses are an important part of the decision, the CB should confirm total cost. All CBs quote day rates (a fee for each assessor day), but there may be other costs, such as application fees, annual management fees, charges for issuing certificates, the assessor's travelling expenses, etc.

The CB can estimate these costs, for the first three years, at the quotation stage. Never just accept the cheapest day rate quote without understanding what will be charged additionally.

Before a formal IMS or EnMS assessment, the CB can provide a gap analysis. This is where a lead assessor will assess the documented EnMs or IMS and provide a written report on whether the organisation is ready for assessment. This can be provided where an organisation already has a certificate for, say, ISO 9001 or more than one standard.

The gap analysis usually takes one or two days but, of course, larger organisations might require a longer period. However, even a one-day gap analysis will give very useful information about whether you are on the right track with your management system in terms of meeting external assessment requirements.

The next step is the assessment itself (sometimes called an extension to scope or change to approval – the CB will confirm).

---

[9] *www.ukas.com/services/accreditation-services/certification-body-accreditation/*.

The duration of the assessment is based on headcount, the number of locations under the proposed certification and risk factors such as the location of the business and the business streams themselves. Although there may be some variation in length, all UKAS-approved CBs should quote around the same duration. They are regulated businesses with reputations to maintain and income streams to protect.

An organisation should remember that the most important cost is the time and opportunity costs within its management team, so the assessment fees are only one element of the budget.

A lead assessor will be appointed by the CB and will contact the organisation – or its consultant – in advance of the assessment to agree an assessment plan. At the end of each assessment a report with a recommendation will be provided.

An assessment is not an exam with a pass mark. All the requirements of an EnMS or IMS will need to be met, although there may be different levels of maturity for different elements of the system.

The assessment will be a combination of interviews and examining of documentary evidence (both electronic and hard copy), which must be available at the assessment. All CBs have a confidentiality agreement process and there should be no need to keep any matters from the lead assessor. Any issues need to be discussed and agreed in advance with the CB, not during the assessment opening meeting.

The lead assessor is not a client or a prospect – the organisation's staff should be candid with them. The lead assessor will test any claims the auditee makes, so prevarication or obfuscation isn't clever commercial negotiation – it can be disastrous for the outcome of an assessment.

Taking an adversarial or fawning approach to a lead assessor is also counterproductive; they may think you are trying to hide something from them. A friendly, professional attitude is ideal. If an organisation really feels that it can't work with the lead assessor assigned, this should be discussed with the CB immediately. Suffering in silence tends to lead to problems later in the assessment process that can be difficult to resolve.

The endgame?

At the end of the assessment, the CB might recommend that an ISO 50001 or IMS certificate be issued, or that it requires further assessment to take place. The assessment recommendation is typically based on the type and number of nonconformities raised. The nonconformities are against the process and the organisation – not against individual directors or members of staff.

Once the ISO 50001 or IMS certificate is issued, a programme of continuing assessments or surveillance visits will be scheduled. Nonconformities can be raised at these visits, and every three years a reassessment takes place.

The endgame isn't getting the certificate but maintaining it. Yet that needn't be an imposition. It is an opportunity to develop the system. The organisation can use its CB as a sounding board and a resource for future plans and challenges – while the CB can't act as a consultant, it can provide added value as part of the standard assessment cost.

FURTHER READING

IT Governance Publishing (ITGP) is the world's leading publisher for governance and compliance. Our industry-leading pocket guides, books, training resources and toolkits are written by real-world practitioners and thought leaders. They are used globally by audiences of all levels, from students to C-suite executives.

Our high-quality publications cover all IT governance, risk and compliance frameworks and are available in a range of formats. This ensures our customers can access the information they need in the way they need it.

Other resources you may find useful include:

- *ISO 50001:2018 Energy Management System (EnMS) Documentation Toolkit,* *www.itgovernancepublishing.co.uk/product/iso-50001-toolkit*
- *Implementing an Integrated Management System (IMS) – The strategic approach* by Alan Field, *www.itgovernancepublishing.co.uk/product/implementing-an-integrated-management-system-ims*
- *ISO 14001 Step by Step – A practical guide, Second edition* by Naeem Sadiq and Asif Hayat Khan, *www.itgovernancepublishing.co.uk/product/iso-14001-step-by-step-a-practical-guide*

For more information on ITGP and branded publishing services, and to view our full list of publications, visit *www.itgovernancepublishing.co.uk*.

To receive regular updates from ITGP, including information on new publications in your area(s) of interest, sign up for our newsletter at *www.itgovernancepublishing.co.uk/topic/newsletter*.

Branded publishing

Through our branded publishing service, you can customise ITGP publications with your company's branding.

Find out more at
www.itgovernancepublishing.co.uk/topic/branded-publishing-services.

Related services

ITGP is part of GRC International Group, which offers a comprehensive range of complementary products and services to help organisations meet their objectives.

For a full range of resources on management systems visit *www.itgovernance.co.uk/shop/category/management-system-standards*.

Training services

The IT Governance training programme is built on our extensive practical experience designing and implementing management systems based on ISO standards, best practice and regulations.

Our courses help attendees develop practical skills and comply with contractual and regulatory requirements. They also support career development via recognised qualifications.

Learn more about our training courses and view the full course catalogue at *www.itgovernance.co.uk/training*.

Professional services and consultancy

We are a leading global consultancy of IT governance, risk management and compliance solutions. We advise businesses around the world on their most critical issues and present cost-saving and risk-reducing solutions based on international best practice and frameworks.

We offer a wide range of delivery methods to suit all budgets, timescales and preferred project approaches.

Further reading

Find out how our consultancy services can help your organisation at *www.itgovernance.co.uk/consulting*.

Industry news

Want to stay up to date with the latest developments and resources in the IT governance and compliance market? Subscribe to our Weekly Round-up newsletter and we will send you mobile-friendly emails with fresh news and features about your preferred areas of interest, as well as unmissable offers and free resources to help you successfully start your projects. *www.itgovernance.co.uk/weekly-round-up*.

EU for product safety is Stephen Evans, The Mill Enterprise Hub, Stagreenan, Drogheda, Co. Louth, A92 CD3D, Ireland. (servicecentre@itgovernance.eu)

www.ingramcontent.com/pod-product-compliance
Lightning Source LLC
Chambersburg PA
CBHW071123210326
41519CB00020B/6399